The Ultimate
Waffle Cookbook

31 Simple and Delicious Waffle Recipes

BY

Gordon Rock

Happy Birthday
Messie!
We hope you enjoy
whipping up batches
of yummy waffles!

♡ Auntie Ke
Uncle Chris
Daniel & Nora 2017

License Notes

No part of this Book can be reproduced in any form or by any means including print, electronic, scanning or photocopying unless prior permission is granted by the author.

All ideas, suggestions and guidelines mentioned here are written for informative purposes. While the author has taken every possible step to ensure accuracy, all readers are advised to follow information at their own risk. The author cannot be held responsible for personal and/or commercial damages in case of misinterpreting and misunderstanding any part of this Book

About the author

Gordon Rock is the author for hundreds of cookbooks on delicious meals that the 'average Joe' can attempt at home. Including, but definitely not limited to, the Amazon Prime bestseller "Smoking Meat: The Essential Guide to Real Barbecue".

Rock is also known for other well-known titles such as "Making Fresh Pasta", "Hot Sauce", "The Paleo Chocolate Lovers" and "Vegan Tacos", just to name a few.

Rock has been nominated for various awards and has recently been offered a 'Question & Answers' column in Food and Wine Magazine that will give him a greater medium to respond to all the queries readers may have after attempting his recipes. He has also been honored by the Institution of Culinary Excellence for his outstanding recipes.

Gordon Rock grew up in the outskirts of Los Angeles in California, where he graduated from the Culinary Institute of America with honors. He still resides there along with his wife and three kids. He operates a non - profit organization for aspiring cooks who are unable to finance their culinary education and spends practically all his spare time either in the kitchen or around his desk writing.

For a complete list of my published books, please, visit my Author's Page...

http://amazon.com/author/gordonrock

You can also check out my blog at: http://grodon-rock.blogspot.com

Or my Facebook Page at:
https://www.facebook.com/ChefGordonRock

Table of Contents

Introduction

Whether you are pulling a frozen waffle out of a toaster during a hectic workweek or whether you are making them from scratch on the weekends, most people believe that the only time that you can enjoy waffles is during breakfast. However, what many people do not know or realize is that waffles have more possibilities than just being enjoyed as a breakfast food. Waffles are not only sweet and savory, but you can enjoy them virtually any time of the day, for breakfast, lunch or dinner.

Waffles in particular hold a special place in the heart of families who love to enjoy a filling home cooked breakfast. Only those who have found themselves plugging in a waffle iron first thing in the morning truly understand the magic that waffles hold from the mouthwatering aromas they emit to the savory taste that sends our taste buds wild.

Waffles are made in such a way that they are just begging to be topped with various things from chocolate chips, to nuts, to fruit. There are endless possibilities to the toppings that you can use and this is just the start of the endless fun that you can have.

When it comes to making waffles, you need to think beyond breakfast and make them with whatever pops into your mind. Whether it is with cheese and corn to make a delicious dinner or ice cream to make a spectacular and decadent dessert. You can even make tasty sandwiches made out of waffles if your let your creativity run wild.

In this book you will find an assortment of creative and great tasting waffle recipes that you can make. You will find festive waffle recipes that you can make just in time for the holiday season or you can put together the most traditional waffle dishes together. Whether you are an avid fan of waffles or want to try your hand at making them, this is certainly the book for you.

So, without further ado let's get started!

Chapter One: The Key Ingredients Needed To Make Waffles

Most of the recipes that you will find in this book call for specific ingredients. Some of the most common ingredients that you will find in these recipes are milk, eggs, flour, vanilla and some kind of leavening agent. In this chapter we will go more in depth into what these ingredients are and what their roles will play in your waffle dishes.

1. Leavening Agents

Some of the common leavening agents that you will use to put together the various waffle recipes listed in this book are baking powder, yeast or baking soda. The primary responsibility of these agents is to help the waffle rise as it cooks, giving it a light and fluffy texture when it is done. I highly recommend using a double acting baking powder. It will begin the leavening process the moment you combine your wet and dry ingredients and will make the fluffiest waffles that you will ever taste.

2. Flours and Grains

The foundation for most of the waffle recipes found in this book is all purpose unbleached flour. The more white flour that you use in a waffle recipe, the lighter the crumb of your waffle will be. However, whole grains as add nutrition, flavor and great texture to your waffles and it is highly recommend that you follow the amount of flour that you have to use to the T.

If you use whole wheat flour, it will add a nutty flavor to your waffles; while buckwheat flour is known for add more crispiness and a darker color to your waffles. On the other hand, using cornmeal will add a particular crunch and sweetness to your waffle. There are a variety of flours and grains out there for your waffle recipes and each one will play a role in the outcome of your dishes.

3. Dairy Products

If flour and grains are considered to be the skin of the waffle, dairy products would be the blood and tissue of your waffles. When you use buttermilk in your recipes, it will give your waffles a subtle tangy flavor, which makes it an excellent match for toppings that are sweet. When you use yogurt or sour cream in your recipes, it will cause your waffles to become rich and tender in texture.

Of course most of the recipes that you will find in this book call for the use of milk, which not only has a lower fat content, but it will still make your waffles fluffy and rich in texture.

4. Mix-In Agents

When it comes to some ingredients that you will use in a few of the waffle recipes I have listed in this cookbook, you will have to mix them in to give the waffles additional flavor and a little kick. Some of the mix-in ingredients that you will use are fresh or frozen fruit. When you add these ingredients you will have to fold them gently in to your batter to ensure even mixing. Some of the ingredients that you will use are fresh blueberries, strawberries, raspberries, coconut or apple. You can also use chocolate, white chocolate or chocolate chips.

5. Maple Syrup

What are waffles without syrup? When it comes to using maple syrup, I recommend that you use only the purest syrup that you can find. Use syrup that is lightly gold in color and that will give your waffles that extra molasses flavor that most of us have come to love.

Chapter Two: Waffle Making Equipment That You Will Need

Of course when it comes to making waffles, you can't just use the basic cooking equipment that you are used to. Waffles recipes call for the use of specialized equipment, but that is nothing more than your standard waffle maker. You will also need some standard measuring equipment, a mixer and some non-stick cooking spray.

In this chapter we will look at the two most popular waffle makers that you can use: The regular waffle maker or a Belgian waffle maker. We will also take a look at other less popular waffle makers so you can decide which maker will be the perfect one for you.

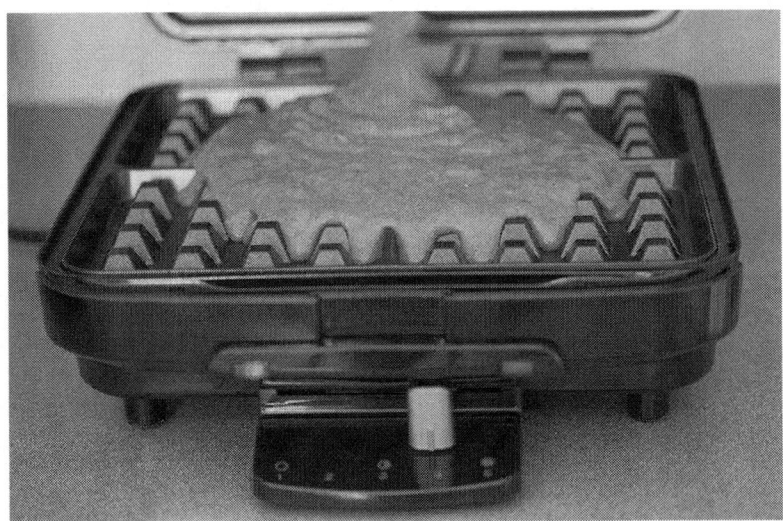

1. Regular Waffle Maker

If you decide to use a standard waffle maker, expect your waffle to come out thin, very crisp and gold in color. These kinds of waffle makers come in a variety of shapes and sizes such as round, square or even heart-shaped. You can even find waffle makers that can cook up to six waffles at a time.

If you go with this traditional waffle maker, I suggest that you find on that has a non-stick cooking plate so that it can make cleaning up and cooking your waffles much easier on you.

2. Belgian Waffle Maker

This type of waffle maker is used to create a variety of waffles, regardless if they are round and square and these waffles will come having large pockets perfect for syrup and toppings as well as high walls on the outer age. Some of these waffle makers can make only one waffle at a time, while a variety of others will prepare up to four waffles at once.

These are the perfect waffle makers to have if you are cooking for a large crowd or want something that makes cooking virtually easier than a traditional waffle maker.

3. The Egg Waffle Maker

This waffle maker makes the sweetest and eggiest of waffles in the particular pattern of spheres, which happens to be one of the most popular street foods in Hong Kong today. These are relatively easy to use, and just like the other waffle makers they come in a variety of shapes and sizes. However, the main different between this maker and the others is that it is made primarily to use for the stove top, preferable over one or two stovetop burners.

Chapter Three: Some Helpful Tips and Tricks

At this point in the game, you are probably very excited to begin cooking your own delicious waffles and you probably want to get started already, but there are just a few extra things that I want to tell you so you can keep them in mind while you are making your waffles. These helpful tips and tricks in this chapter will teach you all of the things that you will learn after cooking waffles for yourself a handful of times, but they will also make the cooking process much easier for you.

Tip #1: Read Your Instruction Manual Carefully

When it comes to using your waffle iron for the very first time, I highly recommend that you read the instruction manual thoroughly, front to back. In the instruction manual you will find different explanations and helps tips such as how to properly grease your waffle iron to what is the best way to clean it.

Tip #2: Different Waffle Makers Will Yield Different Results

As I mentioned in the last chapter, a regular waffle maker will make smaller and thinner waffles, meaning that it will use much less batter to make your waffles. On the other hand, when you use a Belgian waffle maker you will go through much more batter as they tend to make much bigger and fluffier waffles. Keep this in mind as your begin cooking.

Tip #3: Don't Overfill Your Waffle Maker with Batter

I know that it can be tempting to stuff as much batter as you can in your waffle maker, but I am here to advise you against doing this. However, if you accidentally overfill your waffle grids with batter, I recommend that you let the batter cook for a few seconds with the lid of the waffle maker up. Then slowly close the lid to ensure the batter doesn't spill over.

Tip #4: Don't Open the Waffle Maker While It Is Cooking Your Waffles

This is another thing that I know it can be very tempting to do, but just don't do it. Even if you want to take a little peak at your waffles, don't do it! If you are unsure if your waffles are ready, the best indicator for this is to wait until there is no more steam escaping from your waffle iron.

Tip #5: Use Butter or Oil to Grease Your Waffle Iron

If you want to prevent your waffles from sticking to your waffle iron, I highly recommend that you use butter or oil to grease up your iron. Even if your waffles are finished cooking and you are having trouble removing them from the iron, brush some oil or butter along the edges and carefully remove the waffle from the grill.

Always try to grease up your waffle iron thoroughly before each use. This will help ensure that your waffles from out of the iron quickly and easily without sticking or breaking in the process.

Tip #6: Use Rubber Utensils

When it comes to using the right cooking utensils to make your waffles, I highly recommend that you use wooden, rubber or silicone utensils. These utensils will help to remove your waffles from your waffle maker much easier. While you can easily use metal utensils, I advise against this as over time it will remove the non-stick coating of your waffle iron.

Tip #7: How to Get Crispy Waffles Each and Every Time

If you want to get crispy waffles each and every time, I highly recommend putting your finished waffles onto a baking sheet and then baking your waffles in a 300 degree heated oven for about 5 minutes. This will certainly do the trick.

Tip #8: When In Doubt, Make Your Waffles Ahead of Time

Of course waffles that are made fresh right out of the waffle iron tend to be the best tasting waffles; you can make your waffles and then store them for later use. For example if you are making sandwiches later on it the day, prepare your waffles first thing in the morning and then store them in a cool place for later. When you are ready to use them, simply pop them into an oven preheated at 300 degrees and let them warm up for about 5 to 10 minutes. They will come out tasting as if you had just made them.

Tip #9: If You Are Tight On Time, Prepare Everything the Night Before

Most of us work chaotic work schedules and therefore do not have the luxury of time to enjoy a home cooked breakfast in the morning. However, you can still a good and filling breakfast by preparing your batter the night before. Just mix all of your ingredients the night (not together) and store them in your fridge until the next morning. First thing in the morning combine all of your ingredients together and begin making your waffles. It is that simple!

Chapter Four: Delicious Waffle Recipes

This is finally the chapter you have been waiting for. What is a waffle cookbook without a few waffle recipes? In this chapter you will find 40 of the most mouthwatering and delicious waffle recipes that you can make virtually any time of the day, breakfast, lunch or dinner.

So, what are you waiting for? Let's get cooking!

Classic Waffles

To kick things off we will start with the most basic and classic of waffle recipes: the Classic Waffles. With this recipe you can enjoy the ultimate breakfast comfort food with a touch of heaven thrown in.

Makes: 4 to 6 Waffles

Total Prep Time: 20 Minutes

Ingredients:

- 2 Cups of Flour, All Purpose
- 2 Eggs, Large In Size
- 1 ½ Cups of Milk, Whole
- ½ tsp. of Salt
- 1/3 Cup of Butter, Melted
- 4 tsp. of Baking Powder
- 2 Tbsp. of Sugar, White

Directions:

1. Preheat your waffle iron. While your waffle iron is heating up combine all of your dry ingredients together using a large sized mixing bowl until evenly blended together. Set aside.

2. Using a separate bowl beat your eggs until they are fluffy. Then add in your melted butter and milk.

3. Add your egg and milk mixture into your dry ingredient mixture and stir together until thoroughly mixed.

4. Spray your waffle iron with a generous amount of cooking spray. Then ladle some of your waffle batter onto your waffle iron and close the lid. Let your waffles cook until they are crispy and golden in color. Remove and serve with some butter and maple syrup. Enjoy.

Healthy Wholegrain Waffles

If you are looking for a healthy treat, this is certainly the recipe for you. This recipe will make a batch of waffles that are not only incredibly healthy for you, but will leave you craving for more.

Makes: 4 to 6 Waffles

Total Prep Time: 25 Minutes

Ingredients:

- 1 ½ Cups of Flour, All Purpose
- 2 Eggs, Large In Size
- 1 ½ Cups of Milk, Whole
- ½ tsp. of Salt
- 1/3 Cup of Butter, Melted
- 4 tsp. of Baking Powder
- 2 Tbsp. of Sugar, White
- 1 tsp. of Vanilla Extract

Directions:

1. Preheat your waffle iron on the highest setting. While your waffle iron is heating up use a large sized mixing bowl and combine all of your dry ingredients together until evenly mixed. Set this mixture aside.

2. Then using a separate small sized bowl, whisk up your eggs until they are fluffy in consistency. Add in your vanilla extract, melted butter and whole milk and stir to combine.

3. Add your wet mixture to your dry mixture and stir until all of the ingredients are well blended together and smooth in consistency.

4. Spray your waffle iron with a generous amount of cooking spray. Then ladle some of your waffle batter onto your waffle iron and close the lid. Let your waffles cook until they are crispy and golden in color. Remove and I recommend serving them with a cup of chopped up pecans to yield the best results. Enjoy.

Belgian Style Waffles

When it comes to waffles, Belgian style are the absolute best. Now with this recipe you can enjoy these light and fluffy waffles right in the comfort of your own home.

Makes: 6 to 8 Waffles

Total Prep Time: 24 Hours and 20 Minutes

Ingredients:

- 2 Cups of Flour, All Purpose
- 2 Eggs, Large In Size
- 1 ½ Cups of Milk, Whole
- ½ tsp. of Salt
- 1/3 Cup of Butter, Melted
- 1 Pack of Dry Yeast, Active
- 1 tsp. of Vanilla Extract

- 2 Tbsp. of Sugar, White

Directions:

1. Use a large sized mixing bowl and combine all of your dry ingredients except for your dry yeast together until evenly mixed. Set this mixture aside.

2. Then using a separate small sized bowl, whisk up your eggs until they are fluffy in consistency. Add in your vanilla extract, melted butter and whole milk and stir to combine. Last add in your dry yeast and whisk until thoroughly dissolved. Allow your mixture to sit for 5 minutes.

3. Next add your wet ingredients into your dry ingredients and stir to mix everything together. Cover your mixture with plastic wrap and place in your fridge. Allow to chill overnight.

4. The next morning heat up your waffle iron on the highest setting. Spray your waffle iron with a generous amount of cooking spray to grease it up and ladle some of your waffle batter onto it. Close the lid and allow your waffles to cook until they are crispy and golden in color.

5. Remove and serve immediately. I recommend serving these waffles with some whipped cream and fresh strawberries to yield the tastiest results. Enjoy!

Decadent Chocolate Waffles

If you are looking for a change in your breakfast routine, this is the recipe that will certainly do it for you. These decadent waffles are a great treat to enjoy during the week or early on the weekend. It is one recipe that children and adults alike will fall in love with.

Makes: 6 to 8 Waffles

Total Prep Time: 25 Minutes

Ingredients:

- 1 ¾ Cups of Flour, All Purpose
- ½ Cup of Cocoa Powder
- ¼ Cup of Chocolate Chips, Semi-Sweet
- 3 Eggs, Large In Size
- 1 ¾ Cups of Milk, Whole
- ½ tsp. of Salt
- 1/3 Cup of Butter, Melted
- 4 tsp. of Baking Powder
- 1 tsp. of Vanilla Extract
- 2 Tbsp. of Sugar, White

Directions:

1. Preheat your waffle iron. While your waffle iron is heating up combine all of your dry ingredients together using a large sized mixing bowl until evenly blended together. Set aside.

2. Using a separate bowl beat your eggs until they are fluffy. Then add in your melted butter, vanilla extract and milk.

3. Add your egg and milk mixture into your dry ingredient mixture and fold gently together until thoroughly mixed.

4. Spray your waffle iron with a generous amount of cooking spray. Then ladle some of your waffle batter onto your waffle iron and close the lid. Let your waffles cook until they are crispy and golden in color. Remove and serve with some whipped cream and decadent chocolate sauce. Enjoy.

Sweet White Chocolate Waffles

If you are not a big fan of dark chocolate, but are a fan of white chocolate, you are going to fall in love with this recipe. This is a great waffle dish to make if you are looking to change up your breakfast menu and will please even the pickiest of eaters.

Makes: 4 to 6 Waffles

Total Prep Time: 25 Minutes

Ingredients:

- 2 Cups of Flour, All Purpose
- 1/3 Cup of White Chocolate Chips, Miniature
- 3 Eggs, Large In Size
- 1 ¾ Cups of Milk, Whole
- ½ tsp. of Salt
- 1/3 Cup of Butter, Melted
- 4 tsp. of Baking Powder
- 1 tsp. of Vanilla Extract
- 2 Tbsp. of Sugar, White

Directions:

1. Preheat your waffle iron. While your waffle iron is heating up combine all of your dry ingredients together using a large sized mixing bowl until evenly blended together. Set aside.

2. Using a separate bowl beat your eggs until they are fluffy. Then add in your melted butter, vanilla extract and whole milk.

3. Add your egg and milk mixture into your dry ingredient mixture and stir together until thoroughly mixed. Next carefully and gently fold in your white chocolate chips until evenly mixed in.

4. Spray your waffle iron with a generous amount of cooking spray. Then ladle some of your waffle batter onto your waffle iron and close the lid. Let your waffles cook until they are crispy and golden in color. Remove and serve. I recommend serving these waffles with maple syrup and topped with fresh strawberries. Enjoy.

Classic Chocolate Chip Waffles

If you have very young picky eaters that don't want to eat anything for breakfast, you have to try this recipe. This waffle recipe will surely get them excited and will leave them begging for more.

Makes: 6 to 8 Waffles

Total Prep Time: 25 Minutes

Ingredients:

- 2 Cups of Flour, All Purpose
- ¾ Cup of Chocolate Chips, Miniature and Semi-Sweet
- 3 Eggs, Large In Size
- 1 ¾ Cups of Milk, Whole
- ½ tsp. of Salt

- 1/3 Cup of Butter, Melted
- 4 tsp. of Baking Powder
- 1 tsp. of Vanilla Extract
- 2 Tbsp. of Sugar, White

Directions:

1. Preheat your waffle iron on the highest setting. While your waffle iron is heating up use a large sized mixing bowl and combine all of your dry ingredients together until evenly mixed. Set this mixture aside.

2. Then using a separate small sized bowl, whisk up your eggs until they are fluffy in consistency. Add in your vanilla extract, melted butter and whole milk and stir to combine.

3. Add your wet mixture to your dry mixture and stir until all of the ingredients are well blended together and smooth in consistency. Gently and slowly fold in your chocolate chips until evenly combined.

4. Spray your waffle iron with a generous amount of cooking spray. Then ladle some of your waffle batter onto your waffle iron and close the lid. Let your waffles cook until they are crispy and golden in color. Remove and serve. I recommend serving these waffles with a drizzle of chocolate sauce for even tastier results.

Delicious Peanut Butter Waffles

This is yet another great waffle recipe to spring on your kids. What child doesn't enjoy peanut butter? These waffles are a great way to power up your child's day and get them headed out the door on a happy note.

Makes: 4 to 6 Waffles

Total Prep Time: 30 Minutes

Ingredients:

- 2 Cups of Flour, All Purpose
- 2 Eggs, Large In Size
- 1 ½ Cups of Milk, Whole
- 1/3 Cup of Peanut Butter, Smooth
- ½ tsp. of Salt
- 1/3 Cup of Butter, Melted
- 4 tsp. of Baking Powder
- 2 Tbsp. of Sugar, White

Directions:

1. Preheat your waffle iron on the highest setting. While your waffle iron is heating up use a large sized mixing bowl and combine all of your dry ingredients together until evenly mixed. Set this mixture aside.

2. Then using a separate small sized bowl, whisk up your eggs until they are fluffy in consistency. Add in your smooth peanut butter, melted butter and whole milk and stir to combine.

3. Add your wet mixture to your dry mixture and stir until all of the ingredients are well blended together and smooth in consistency.

4. Spray your waffle iron with a generous amount of cooking spray. Then ladle some of your waffle batter onto your waffle iron and close the lid. Let your waffles cook until they are crispy and golden in color. Remove and serve. I recommend serving these tasty waffles with some fresh strawberry jam for a real tasty treat.

Healthy Banana Waffles

In my opinion, bananas can go with virtually anything and that applies with this recipe. These waffles can make a great tasty snack or a fulfilling breakfast meal.

Makes: 4 to 6 Waffles

Total Prep Time: 20 Minutes

Ingredients:

- 2 Cups of Flour, All Purpose
- 2 Eggs, Large In Size
- 1 ½ Cups of Milk, Whole
- ½ tsp. of Salt
- 1/3 Cup of Butter, Melted
- 4 tsp. of Baking Powder
- 1 tsp. of Vanilla Extract

- 2 Tbsp. of Sugar, White
- 2 Bananas, Ripe and Mashed
- ½ tsp. of Cinnamon, Ground

Directions:

1. Preheat your waffle iron on the highest setting. While your waffle iron is heating up use a large sized mixing bowl and combine all of your dry ingredients together until evenly mixed. Set this mixture aside.

2. Then using a separate small sized bowl, whisk up your eggs until they are fluffy in consistency. Add in your vanilla extract, melted butter, mashed bananas and whole milk and stir to combine.

3. Add your wet mixture to your dry mixture and stir until all of the ingredients are well blended together and smooth in consistency.

4. Spray your waffle iron with a generous amount of cooking spray. Then ladle some of your waffle batter onto your waffle iron and close the lid. Let your waffles cook until they are crispy and golden in color. Remove and I recommend serving them with a cup of your favorite chopped nuts to yield the best results. Enjoy.

Norwegian Style Waffles

This is a great recipe to make if you are looking to bring a little culture into your kitchen. These waffles are gold in color and crispy to taste, making them the perfect go-to food when you are looking for something to fill you up before your busy day.

Makes: 6 to 8

Total Prep Time: 20 Minutes

Ingredients:

- 2 Cups of Flour, All Purpose
- 3 Eggs, Large In Size
- 1 Cup of Buttermilk
- ½ Cup of Milk, Whole
- ½ tsp. of Salt
- 1/3 Cup of Butter, Melted
- 4 tsp. of Baking Powder
- ½ Cup of Sugar, White

Directions:

1. Preheat your waffle iron on the highest setting. While your waffle iron is heating up use a large sized mixing bowl and combine all of your dry ingredients together until evenly mixed. Set this mixture aside.

2. Then using a separate small sized bowl, whisk up your eggs until they are fluffy in consistency. Add in your buttermilk, melted butter and whole milk and stir to combine.

3. Add your wet mixture to your dry mixture and stir until all of the ingredients are well blended together and smooth

4. Spray your waffle iron with a generous amount of cooking spray. Then ladle some of your waffle batter onto your waffle iron and close the lid. Let your waffles cook until they are crispy and golden in color. Remove and serve them with some warm butter and your favorite kind of maple syrup.

Classic Blueberry Waffles

If you are looking for a traditional and relatively easy waffle recipe to make, this recipe is the one for. This recipe is incredibly simple to put together and are bursting with delicious blueberry flavor with every bite.

Makes: 4 to 6 Waffles

Total Prep Time: 25 Minutes

Ingredients:

- 2 Cups of Flour, All Purpose
- 1 Cup of Blueberries, Fresh
- 3 Eggs, Large In Size
- 1 ¾ Cup of Milk, Whole
- ½ tsp. of Salt
- 1/3 Cup of Butter, Melted
- 4 tsp. of Baking Powder
- 2 Tbsp. of Sugar, White

Directions:

1. Preheat your waffle iron. While your waffle iron is heating up combine all of your dry ingredients together using a large sized mixing bowl until evenly blended together. Set aside.

2. Using a separate bowl beat your eggs until they are fluffy. Then add in your melted butter and whole milk.

3. Add your egg and milk mixture into your dry ingredient mixture and fold gently together until thoroughly mixed. Then add in your fresh blueberries and fold them into your mixture with great care.

4. Spray your waffle iron with a generous amount of cooking spray. Then ladle some of your waffle batter onto your waffle iron and close the lid. Let your waffles cook until they are crispy and golden in color. Remove and serve with some of your favorite brand of maple syrup and enjoy.

Tasty and Fresh Apple Waffles

Apples are one of the best ingredients to add to any breakfast recipe that can enhance the flavor of virtually any dish.

Makes: 6 to 8 Waffles

Total Prep Time: 25 Minutes

Ingredients:

- 2 Cups of Flour, All Purpose
- 2 Eggs, Large In Size
- 1 ½ Cups of Milk, Whole
- ½ tsp. of Salt
- 1/3 Cup of Butter, Melted
- 4 tsp. of Baking Powder
- 1 tsp. of Vanilla Extract

- 2 Tbs. of Sugar, White
- 1 ½ Cups of Apples, Granny Smith, Peeled and Grated

Directions:

1. Preheat your waffle iron. While your waffle iron is heating up combine all of your dry ingredients together using a large sized mixing bowl until evenly blended together. Set aside.

2. Using a separate bowl beat your eggs until they are fluffy. Then add in your melted butter, vanilla extract and milk.

3. Add your egg and milk mixture into your dry ingredient mixture and fold gently together until thoroughly mixed. Next fold in your grated apples gently until the mixture is relatively smooth.

4. Spray your waffle iron with a generous amount of cooking spray. Then ladle some of your waffle batter onto your waffle iron and close the lid. Let your waffles cook until they are crispy and golden in color. Remove and serve with some of your favorite kind of maple syrup. Enjoy.

Crazy Triple Berry Waffles

This is one waffle recipe that you will not forget anytime soon. Packed with three different kinds of berries, you can rest assured that your taste buds will be assaulted by a variety of unique and tasty flavors.

Makes: 6 to 8 Waffles

Total Prep Time: 20 Minutes

Ingredients:

- 2 Cups of Flour, All Purpose
- ¼ Cups of Blueberries, Fresh
- ¼ Cups of Strawberries, Fresh and Chopped Roughly
- ¼ Cups of Raspberries, Fresh and Chopped Roughly

- 3 Eggs, Large In Size
- 1 ¾ Cups of Milk, Whole
- ½ tsp. of Salt
- 1/3 Cups of Butter, Melted
- 4 tsp. of Baking Powder
- 2 Tbsp. of Sugar, White

Directions:

1. Preheat your waffle iron. While your waffle iron is heating up combine all of your dry ingredients together using a large sized mixing bowl until evenly blended together. Set aside.

2. Using a separate bowl beat your eggs until they are fluffy. Then add in your melted butter and milk.

3. Add your egg and milk mixture into your dry ingredient mixture and fold gently together until thoroughly mixed. Add in each of berries one at a time and blend until your batter is relatively smooth in consistency.

4. Spray your waffle iron with a generous amount of cooking spray. Then ladle some of your waffle batter onto your waffle iron and close the lid. Let your waffles cook until they are crispy and golden in color. Remove and serve immediately. Enjoy!

Orange Flavored Waffles

These waffles are sure to wake you up in the morning! Bursting with flavor and easy to make, these are some of the tastiest waffles that you will ever get the chance to enjoy.

Makes: 4 to 6 Waffles

Total Prep Time: 20 Minutes

Ingredients:

- 2 Cups of Flour, All Purpose
- 2 Eggs, Large In Size
- ½ Cup of Milk, Whole
- 1 Cup of Orange Juice, No Pulp

- ½ tsp. of Salt
- 1/3 Cup of Butter, Melted
- 4 tsp. of Baking Powder
- 2 Tbsp. of Sugar, White
- 2 Tbsp. of Orange Zest

Directions:

1. Preheat your waffle iron. While your waffle iron is heating up combine all of your dry ingredients together including your orange zest using a large sized mixing bowl until evenly blended together. Set aside.

2. Using a separate bowl beat your eggs until they are fluffy. Then add in your melted butter, orange juice and whole milk.

3. Add your egg and milk mixture into your dry ingredient mixture and gently beat together until thoroughly mixed.

4. Spray your waffle iron with a generous amount of cooking spray. Then ladle some of your waffle batter onto your waffle iron and close the lid. Let your waffles cook until they are crispy and golden in color. Remove and serve.

If you want to add some extra zest to your waffles, don't hesitate to add more orange zest into the batter.

Mouthwatering Maple Bacon Waffles

What is our world without bacon? Bacon goes with virtually any breakfast item and now you can prepare waffles with bacon cooked right into them. What could be better than that?

Makes: 4 to 6 Waffles

Total Prep Time: 25 Minutes

Ingredients:

- 2 Cups of Flour, All Purpose
- 2 Eggs, Large In Size
- 1 ½ Cups of Milk, Whole
- ½ tsp. of Salt
- 1/3 Cup of Butter, Melted
- 4 tsp. of Baking Powder
- 2 Tbsp. of Sugar, White
- ¼ Cup of Maple Syrup, Pure and You're Favorite Brand
- 4 Slices of Bacon, Fully Cooked and Crumbled

Directions:

1. Preheat your waffle iron. While your waffle iron is heating up combine all of your dry ingredients together using a large sized mixing bowl until evenly blended together. Set aside.

2. Using a separate bowl beat your eggs until they are fluffy. Then add in your melted butter, maple syrup and whole milk. Stir until evenly combined. Fold in your bacon gently.

3. Add your egg and milk mixture into your dry ingredient mixture and stir together until thoroughly mixed.

4. Spray your waffle iron with a generous amount of cooking spray. Then ladle some of your waffle batter onto your waffle iron and close the lid. Let your waffles cook until they are crispy and golden in color. Remove and serve with some butter and maple syrup. Enjoy.

Classic Buttermilk Waffles

Just like with pancakes, buttermilk adds great flavor to traditional waffles and helps to add a little extra crisp to them. With this recipe you can enjoy a classic waffle recipe that will remind you of your own mother's home cooked meals.

Makes: 6 to 8 Waffles

Total Prep Time: 20 Minutes

Ingredients:

- 2 Cups of Flour, All Purpose
- 3 Eggs, Large In Size
- 1 Cup of Buttermilk
- ½ Cup of Milk, Whole
- ½ tsp. of Salt
- 1/3 Cup of Butter, Melted
- 4 tsp. of Baking Powder
- ½ Cup of Sugar, White

Directions:

1. Preheat your waffle iron. While your waffle iron is heating up combine all of your dry ingredients together using a large sized mixing bowl until evenly blended together. Set aside.

2. Using a separate bowl beat your eggs until they are fluffy. Then add in your melted butter, buttermilk and whole milk.

3. Add your egg and milk mixture into your dry ingredient mixture and stir together until thoroughly mixed and smooth in consistency.

4. Spray your waffle iron with a generous amount of cooking spray. Then ladle some of your waffle batter onto your waffle iron and close the lid. Let your waffles cook until they are crispy and golden in color. Remove and serve with some butter and maple syrup. Enjoy.

Tasty Tiramisu Waffles

With this waffle recipe you won't be able to tell if you are eating the dessert or eating a tasty breakfast. These waffles are that good!

Makes: 4 to 6 Waffles

Total Prep Time: 30 Minutes

Ingredients:

- 1 ¾ Cups of Flour, All Purpose
- ½ Cup of Cocoa Powder, Unsweetened
- 1 tsp. of Cinnamon, Ground
- 2 Tbsp. of Coffee, Strong
- 1 Tbsp. of Brandy, Optional
- 3 Eggs, Large In Size
- 1 ¾ Cups of Milk, Whole
- ½ tsp. of Salt
- 1/3 Cup of Butter, Melted
- 4 tsp. of Baking Powder
- 2 tsp. of Vanilla Extract
- 2 Tbsp. of Sugar, White
- ½ Cup of Mascarpone Cheese
- ½ Cup of Sugar, Powdered
- ½ Cup of Heavy Cream

Directions:

1. Preheat your waffle iron. While your waffle iron is heating up combine all of your dry ingredients together using a large sized mixing bowl until evenly blended together. Set aside.

2. Using a separate bowl beat your eggs until they are fluffy. Then add in your melted butter, coffee, brandy (if you are using it) and milk.

3. Add your egg and milk mixture into your dry ingredient mixture and stir together until thoroughly mixed.

4. Spray your waffle iron with a generous amount of cooking spray. Then ladle some of your waffle batter onto your waffle iron and close the lid. Let your waffles cook until they are crispy and golden in color. Remove.

5. While your waffles are cooking, beat together your cheese, powdered sugar, heavy cream and some extra vanilla together with a blender until small and stiff peaks begin to form on the surface.

6. Serve your waffles with your whipped mascarpone whipped cream served on top and enjoy immediately. For tastier waffles, sprinkle some of your powdered coffee on top of your waffles.

Delicious Fresh Strawberries Waffles

We have covered apple, blueberry and triple berry waffles. Now it is time to cover strawberries. With this recipe you will be able to enjoy tasty waffles with fresh strawberries baked right into them.

Makes: 6 to 8 Waffles

Total Prep Time: 20 Minutes

Ingredients:

- 2 Cups of Flour, All Purpose
- 1 Cup of Strawberries, Fresh and Chopped Finely
- 3 Eggs, Large In Size
- 1 ¾ Cups of Milk, Whole
- ½ tsp. of Salt
- 1/3 Cup of Butter, Melted
- 4 tsp. of Baking Powder
- 2 Tbsp. of Sugar, White

Directions:

1. Preheat your waffle iron. While your waffle iron is heating up combine all of your dry ingredients together using a large sized mixing bowl until evenly blended together. Set aside.

2. Using a separate bowl beat your eggs until they are fluffy. Then add in your melted butter and milk.

3. Add your egg and milk mixture into your dry ingredient mixture and stir together until thoroughly mixed. Gently fold in your fresh strawberries until relatively smooth in consistency.

4. Spray your waffle iron with a generous amount of cooking spray. Then ladle some of your waffle batter onto your waffle iron and close the lid. Let your waffles cook until they are crispy and golden in color. Remove and serve with some butter and maple syrup. Enjoy.

Savory Nutella Waffles

With Nutella being one of the most popular spread today, I couldn't leave this recipe out of this book! Nutella is a great addition to breakfast waffles and once you try it for yourself, you will never be able to eat traditional waffles again.

Makes: 3 to 4 Waffles

Total Prep Time: 25 Minutes

Ingredients:

- 2 Cups of Flour, All Purpose
- 2 Eggs, Large In Size
- 1 ½ Cups of Milk, Whole
- 1/3 Cup of Nutella, Your Favorite Kind and Variety
- ½ tsp. of Salt
- 1/3 Cup of Butter, Melted
- 4 tsp. of Baking Powder
- 2 Tbsp. of Sugar, White

Directions:

1. Preheat your waffle iron on the highest setting. While your waffle iron is heating up use a large sized mixing bowl and combine all of your dry ingredients together until evenly mixed. Set this mixture aside.

2. Then using a separate small sized bowl, whisk up your eggs until they are fluffy in consistency. Add in your Nutella, melted butter and whole milk and stir to combine.

3. Add your wet mixture to your dry mixture and stir until all of the ingredients are well blended together and smooth in consistency.

4. Spray your waffle iron with a generous amount of cooking spray. Then ladle some of your waffle batter onto your waffle iron and close the lid. Let your waffles cook until they are crispy and golden in color. Remove and serve with a sprinkling of powdered sugar. Enjoy!

Pecan Chocolate Chip Waffles

If you are looking for an especially sweet and tasty breakfast recipe, this is the recipe for you. These waffles are stuffed with pecans and chocolate chips, giving you a tasty treat that is sure to please your sweet tooth.

Makes: 3 to 4 Waffles

Total Prep Time: 20 Minutes

Ingredients:

- 2 Cups of Flour, All Purpose
- ½ Cup of Chocolate Chips, Miniature and Semi-Sweet
- ½ Cup of Pecans, Chopped Finely
- 3 Eggs, Large In Size
- 1 ¾ Cups of Milk, Whole

- ½ tsp. of Salt
- 1/3 Cup of Butter, Melted
- 4 tsp. of Baking Powder
- 1 tsp. of Vanilla Extract
- 2 Tbsp. of Sugar, White

Directions:

1. Preheat your waffle iron on the highest setting. While your waffle iron is heating up use a large sized mixing bowl and combine all of your dry ingredients together until evenly mixed. Set this mixture aside.

2. Then using a separate small sized bowl, whisk up your eggs until they are fluffy in consistency. Add in your vanilla extract, melted butter and whole milk and stir to combine.

3. Add your wet mixture to your dry mixture and stir until all of the ingredients are well blended together and smooth in consistency. Fold in your chocolate chips and chopped pecans individually and very gently until thoroughly combined with your batter.

4. Spray your waffle iron with a generous amount of cooking spray. Then ladle some of your waffle batter onto your waffle iron and close the lid. Let your waffles cook until they are crispy and golden in color. Remove and serve.

To enjoy even tastier results, serve these waffles with a dollop or more of whipped cream.

Gingerbread Flavored Waffles

Want to spice up your holidays and get your entire family excited for the holiday season? Then you have got to try this recipe. It is packed full of warm spices and is a great one to make to celebrate the holidays.

Makes: 4 to 6 Waffles

Total Prep Time: 30 Minutes

Ingredients:

- 2 Cups of Flour, All Purpose
- 2 Eggs, Large In Size
- 1 ½ Cups of Milk, Whole
- ½ tsp. of Salt
- 1/3 Cup of Butter, Melted
- 4 tsp. of Baking Powder

- 2 Tbsp. of Sugar, White
- 1 tsp. of Ginger, Ground
- ½ tsp. of Cinnamon, Ground
- ¼ tsp. of Nutmeg, Ground
- ¼ tsp. of Cloves, Ground
- ½ Cup of Molasses

Directions:

1. Preheat your waffle iron on the highest setting. While your waffle iron is heating up use a large sized mixing bowl and combine all of your dry ingredients together until evenly mixed. Set this mixture aside.

2. Then using a separate small sized bowl, whisk up your eggs until they are fluffy in consistency. Add in your molasses, melted butter and whole milk and stir to combine.

3. Add your wet mixture to your dry mixture and stir until all of the ingredients are well blended together and smooth in consistency.

4. Spray your waffle iron with a generous amount of cooking spray. Then ladle some of your waffle batter onto your waffle iron and close the lid. Let your waffles cook until they are crispy and golden in color. Remove and serve immediately with some molasses drizzled over the top. Enjoy!

Beer Battered Waffles

If you have ever had a beer battered burger and looked how the beer seems to gives that burger an extra kick, you are going to love this recipe. The beer that is used acts like a yeast, making these waffles the fluffiest you will ever see or taste.

Makes: 4 to 6

Total Prep Time: 20 Minutes

Ingredients:

- 2 Cups of Flour, All Purpose
- 12 Ounces of Beer, Dark Preferable
- 2 Eggs, Large In Size
- ½ Cup of Milk
- ½ tsp. of Salt
- 1/3 Cup of Butter, Melted
- 4 tsp. of Baking Powder
- 2 Tbsp. of Honey, Raw

Directions:

1. Preheat your waffle iron on the highest setting. While your waffle iron is heating up use a large sized mixing bowl and combine all of your dry ingredients together until evenly mixed. Set this mixture aside.

2. Then using a separate small sized bowl, whisk up your eggs until they are fluffy in consistency. Add in your beer, melted butter, raw honey and whole milk and stir to combine.

3. Add your wet mixture to your dry mixture and stir until all of the ingredients are well blended together and smooth in consistency.

4. Spray your waffle iron with a generous amount of cooking spray. Then ladle some of your waffle batter onto your waffle iron and close the lid. Let your waffles cook until they are crispy and golden in color. Remove and serve. I recommend serving these waffles with extra honey poured over the top of them and a side of fruit.

Decadent Apple Pie Waffles

Fan of apple pie? Then you are going to drool over this recipe. These waffles taste just like the real thing that you will not be able to tell the difference. This is a recipe that you and the entire family are going to want to make again and again.

Makes: 4 to 6 Waffles

Total Prep Time: 25 Minutes

Ingredients:

- 1 ½ Cups of Flour, All Purpose
- ½ Cup of Wheat Bran
- 2 Eggs, Large In Size
- 1 ½ Cups of Milk, Whole
- ½ tsp. of Salt

- 1/3 Cup of Butter, Melted
- 4 tsp. of Baking Powder
- 1 tsp. of Vanilla Extract
- 2 Tbsp. of Sugar, White
- 1 tsp. of Apple Pie Spice
- 1 ½ Cups of Apples, Granny Smith, Peeled and Grated Finely

Directions:

1. Preheat your waffle iron on the highest setting. While your waffle iron is heating up use a large sized mixing bowl and combine all of your dry ingredients together until evenly mixed. Set this mixture aside.

2. Then using a separate small sized bowl, whisk up your eggs until they are fluffy in consistency. Add in your vanilla extract, melted butter and whole milk and stir to combine.

3. Add your wet mixture to your dry mixture and stir until all of the ingredients are well blended together and smooth in consistency. Gently fold in your finely grated apples until thoroughly combined.

4. Spray your waffle iron with a generous amount of cooking spray. Then ladle some of your waffle batter onto your waffle iron and close the lid. Let your waffles cook until they are crispy and golden in color. Remove and serve immediately. I recommend serving these waffles with a generous helping of whipped cream. Enjoy.

Festive Eggnog Waffles

Here is yet another tasty recipe that you can enjoy for the holidays. Whether you serve this dish on Thanksgiving or on Christmas Eve, everybody who gets a bite of these waffles will surely fall in love with them.

Makes: 3 to 4 Waffles

Total Prep Time: 25 Minutes

Ingredients:

- 2 Cups of Flour, All Purpose
- 2 Eggs, Large In Size
- 1 Cup of Eggnog, Your Favorite Brand or Homemade
- ½ Cup of Milk, Whole
- ½ tsp. of Salt
- 1/3 Cup of Butter, Melted
- 4 tsp. of Baking Powder
- 2 Tbsp. of Sugar, White
- 1 tsp. of Ginger, Ground
- ½ tsp. of Cinnamon, Ground
- ¼ tsp. of Nutmeg, Ground
- ¼ tsp. of Cloves, Ground
- ½ Cup of Molasses

Directions:

1. Preheat your waffle iron on the highest setting. While your waffle iron is heating up use a large sized mixing bowl and combine all of your dry ingredients together including your spices until evenly mixed. Set this mixture aside.

2. Then using a separate small sized bowl, whisk up your eggs until they are fluffy in consistency. Add in your eggnog, molasses, melted butter and whole milk and stir to combine.

3. Add your wet mixture to your dry mixture and stir until all of the ingredients are well blended together and smooth in consistency.

4. Spray your waffle iron with a generous amount of cooking spray. Then ladle some of your waffle batter onto your waffle iron and close the lid. Let your waffles cook until they are crispy and golden in color. Remove and serve at once. For the best results I recommend serving these waffles with just a dash of cinnamon sprinkled over the top and a generous amount of maple syrup.

Healthy Zucchini Waffles

Yet another healthy and great recipe, these waffles are a breakfast item that you are surely going to enjoy. This recipe is a great way to sneak some veggies into your kid's diet without them even noticing it.

Makes: 4 to 6 Waffles

Total Prep Time: 20 Minutes

Ingredients:

- 1 ½ Cups of Flour, Whole Wheat
- 2 Eggs, Large In Size
- 1 ½ Cups of Milk, Whole
- ½ tsp. of Salt
- 1/3 Cup of Butter, Melted
- 4 tsp. of Baking Powder
- 2 Tbsp. of Sugar, White
- 1 tsp. of Vanilla Extract, Pure
- 1 Cup of Zucchini, Shredded and Patted Dry
- 1 tsp. of Cinnamon, Ground

Directions:

1. Preheat your waffle iron on the highest setting. While your waffle iron is heating up use a large sized mixing bowl and combine all of your dry ingredients together until evenly mixed. Set this mixture aside.

2. Then using a separate small sized bowl, whisk up your eggs until they are fluffy in consistency. Add in your vanilla extract, butter and milk and stir to combine.

3. Add your wet mixture to your dry mixture and stir until all of the ingredients are well blended together and smooth in consistency. Next gently fold in your shredded zucchini until mixed well in your batter.

4. Spray your waffle iron with a generous amount of cooking spray. Then ladle some of your waffle batter onto your waffle iron and close the lid. Let your waffles cook until they are crispy and golden in color. Remove and serve with a generous amount of butter and syrup. Enjoy.

Yummy Oatmeal Waffles

If you are a fan of oatmeal cookies, this is one recipe that you are certainly going to enjoy. Incredibly simple to put together and packed with amazing taste, these waffles will soon become a household favorite in no time

Makes: 6 to 8 Waffles

Total Prep Time: 25 Minutes

Ingredients:

- 1 ½ Cups of Flour, All Purpose
- 1 Cup of Oats, Quick Cooking Variety
- 1 tsp. of Cinnamon, Ground
- 2 Eggs, Large In Size
- 1 ½ Cups of Milk
- ½ tsp. of Salt
- 1/3 Cup of Butter, Melted
- 4 tsp. of Baking Powder
- 2 Tbsp. of Sugar, White

Directions:

1. Preheat your waffle iron on the highest setting. While your waffle iron is heating up use a large sized mixing bowl and combine all of your dry ingredients together until evenly mixed. Set this mixture aside.

2. Then using a separate small sized bowl, whisk up your eggs until they are fluffy in consistency. Add in your melted butter and whole milk and stir to combine.

3. Add your wet mixture to your dry mixture and stir until all of the ingredients are well blended together and smooth in consistency.

4. Spray your waffle iron with a generous amount of cooking spray. Then ladle some of your waffle batter onto your waffle iron and close the lid. Let your waffles cook until they are crispy and golden in color. Remove and serve at once. Enjoy!

Coconut Flavored Waffles

There are many people out there that absolutely love the taste of coconut. If you are an avid fan of coconut, then this recipe is especially for you. These waffles are relatively easy to make and will be gone before you know it.

Makes: 4 to 6 Waffles

Total Prep Time: 20 Minutes

Ingredients:

- 1 ¾ Cups of Flour, All Purpose
- 1 Cup of Coconut, Unsweetened and Shredded
- 2 Eggs, Large In Size
- 1 Cup of Milk, Whole
- ½ Cup of Coconut Milk, Unsweetened
- ½ tsp. of Salt
- 1/3 Cup of Butter, Melted
- 4 tsp. of Baking Powder
- 2 Tbsp. of Sugar, White

Directions:

1. Preheat your waffle iron. While your waffle iron is heating up combine all of your dry ingredients together including your shredded coconut using a large sized mixing bowl until evenly blended together. Set aside.

2. Using a separate bowl beat your eggs until they are fluffy. Then add in your melted butter, coconut milk and whole milk.

3. Add your egg and milk mixture into your dry ingredient mixture and stir together until thoroughly mixed.

4. Spray your waffle iron with a generous amount of cooking spray. Then ladle some of your waffle batter onto your waffle iron and close the lid. Let your waffles cook until they are crispy and golden in color. Remove and serve. I recommend serving these waffles with a drizzle of chocolate syrup to yield tastier results. Enjoy!

Bacon and Cheese Stuffed Waffles

If you are looking for the perfect breakfast on the go that will taste just as amazing as if you were sitting in a diner, then you have to try this recipe! Stuffed full of bacon and cheese, with these waffles you can just pop them in the toaster right before you are heading out of the door.

Makes: 3 to 4 Waffles

Total Prep Time: 20 Minutes

Ingredients:

- 2 Cups of Flour, All Purpose
- 2 Eggs, Large In Size
- 1 ½ Cups of Milk, Whole
- ½ tsp. of Salt
- 1/3 Cup of Butter, Melted
- 4 tsp. of Baking Powder
- 2 Tbsp. of Sugar, White
- 8 Slices of Bacon, Fully Cooked and Crumbled
- ½ Cup of Cheddar Cheese, Shredded

Directions:

1. Preheat your waffle iron. While your waffle iron is heating up combine all of your dry ingredients together using a large sized mixing bowl until evenly blended together. Set aside.

2. Using a separate bowl beat your eggs until they are fluffy. Then add in your butter and milk.

3. Add your egg and milk mixture into your dry ingredient mixture and stir together until thoroughly mixed.

4. Spray your waffle iron with a generous amount of cooking spray. Then ladle some of your waffle batter onto your waffle iron and close the lid. Let your waffles cook until they are crispy and golden in color. Remove and serve. I recommend serving these waffles with maple syrup and butter.

Nutmeg Battered Waffles

These recipes will surely give you waffles that have a little extra kick to them. These waffles are the ultimate comfort food and the added nutmeg gives these waffles that little extra spice that you have been looking for.

Makes: 4 to 6 Waffles

Total Prep Time: 25 Minutes

Ingredients:

- 2 Cups of Flour, All Purpose
- 2 Eggs, Large In Size
- 1 ½ Cups of Milk, Whole
- ½ tsp. of Salt
- 1/3 Cup of Butter, Melted
- 4 tsp. of Baking Powder
- 2 Tbsp. of Sugar, White
- 1 tsp. of Nutmeg, Fresh and Grated
- 1 tsp. of Vanilla Extract

Directions:

1. Preheat your waffle iron. While your waffle iron is heating up combine all of your dry ingredients together using a large sized mixing bowl until evenly blended together. Set aside.

2. Using a separate bowl beat your eggs until they are fluffy. Then add in your melted butter, vanilla extract and whole milk.

3. Add your egg and milk mixture into your dry ingredient mixture and stir together until thoroughly mixed.

4. Spray your waffle iron with a generous amount of cooking spray. Then ladle some of your waffle batter onto your waffle iron and close the lid. Let your waffles cook until they are crispy and golden in color. Remove and serve. I recommend serving these waffles with some syrup and fresh blueberries.

Chocolate Dipped Waffles

These tasty waffles are extremely crispy and are great if you are suffering from a strong sweet tooth. Dip these waffles in some decadent chocolate to have the ultimate snack.

Makes: 3 to 4 Waffles

Total Prep Time: 20 Minutes

Ingredients:

- 2 Cups of Flour, All Purpose
- 2 Eggs, Large In Size
- 1 ½ Cups of Milk, Whole
- 1 tsp. of Cinnamon, Ground
- 1 tsp. of Vanilla Extract
- ½ tsp. Salt
- 1/3 Cup of Butter, Melted
- 4 tsp. of Baking Powder
- 2 Tbsp. of Sugar, White
- 1 Cup of Chocolate Chips, Semi Sweet
- 1 tsp. of Shortening

Directions:

1. Preheat your waffle iron. While your waffle iron is heating up combine all of your dry ingredients together using a large sized mixing bowl until evenly blended together. Set aside.

2. Using a separate bowl beat your eggs until they are fluffy. Then add in your melted butter, vanilla extract and whole milk.

3. Add your egg and milk mixture into your dry ingredient mixture and stir together until thoroughly mixed.

4. Next melt your chocolate chips and shortening together in your microwave. Stir.

5. Spray your waffle iron with a generous amount of cooking spray. Then ladle some of your waffle batter onto your waffle iron and close the lid. Let your waffles cook until they are crispy and golden in color. Remove and cut up your waffles into quarters and dip them in your melted chocolate. Enjoy!

Tasty Herb Waffles

These waffles can be made to accompany a heart stew or soup recipe. They are incredibly easy to make and make for a quick dinner fix.

Makes: 6 to 8 Waffles

Total Prep Time: 30 Minutes

Ingredients:

- 2 Cups of Flour, All Purpose
- 2 Eggs, Large
- 1 Cup of Milk, Whole
- ½ Cup of Sour Cream
- ½ tsp. of Salt
- 1 tsp. of Garlic, Powder
- 1 tsp. of Parsley, Dried
- ½ tsp. of Rosemary, Dried
- ¼ tsp. of Tarragon, Dried
- 1/3 Cup of Butter, Melted
- 4 tsp. of Baking Powder

Directions:

1. Preheat your waffle iron. While your waffle iron is heating up combine all of your dry ingredients together using a large sized mixing bowl until evenly blended together including your dried herbs. Set aside.

2. Using a separate bowl beat your eggs until they are fluffy. Then add in your melted butter, vanilla extract and whole milk.

3. Add your egg and milk mixture into your dry ingredient mixture and stir together until thoroughly mixed.

4. Spray your waffle iron with a generous amount of cooking spray. Then ladle some of your waffle batter onto your waffle iron and close the lid. Let your waffles cook until they are crispy and golden in color. Remove and serve immediately.

Sweet Maple Walnut Waffles

These waffles are incredibly sweet and will satisfy any sweet tooth. Crispy on the outside and soft one the inside, these waffles make the ultimate treat for breakfast, lunch or dinner.

Makes: 3 to 4 Waffles

Total Prep Time: 20 Minutes

Ingredients:

- 2 Cups of Flour, All Purpose
- 2 Eggs, Large In Size
- 1 ½ Cups of Milk, Whole
- ½ tsp. of Salt
- 1/3 Cup of Butter, Melted
- 4 tsp. of Baking Powder
- 2 Tbsp. of Sugar, White
- ¼ Cup of Maple Syrup, Pure
- ½ Cup of Walnuts, Finely Chopped

Directions:

1. Preheat your waffle iron. While your waffle iron is heating up combine all of your dry ingredients together using a large sized mixing bowl until evenly blended together. Set aside.

2. Using a separate bowl beat your eggs until they are fluffy. Then add in your melted butter, vanilla extract and whole milk.

3. Add your egg and milk mixture into your dry ingredient mixture and stir together until thoroughly mixed. Next carefully and gently fold in your chopped walnuts until evenly mixed in.

4. Spray your waffle iron with a generous amount of cooking spray. Then ladle some of your waffle batter onto your waffle iron and close the lid. Let your waffles cook until they are crispy and golden in color. Remove and serve. I recommend serving these waffles with maple syrup and butter. Enjoy!

Conclusion

There you have it! Hopefully with this book you have learned not only what it takes to make the best tasting waffles ever, but have also learned about the different equipment that you need and the different types of ingredients that are most commonly found in waffle recipes today.

The next thing for you to do is begin making all of the tasty waffle recipes that are in this book so you can become the master waffle maker you have always wanted to be. Remember, take it slow and have fun when making your waffles. Don't hesitate to get creative with these recipes and add in whatever extra ingredients or toppings that you want.

Good luck and happy cooking!

Author's Afterthoughts

Thanks ever so much to each of my cherished readers for investing the time to read this book!

I know you could have picked from many other books but you chose this one. So a big thanks for downloading this book and reading all the way to the end.

If you enjoyed this book or received value from it, I'd like to ask you for a favor. Please take a few minutes to post an honest and heartfelt review on Amazon.com. Your support does make a difference and helps to benefit other people.

Thanks for your Reviews!

Gordon Rock
bunsomsaetow@gmail.com

Made in the USA
Middletown, DE
01 August 2017